Contents

Prologue.. P.2
    Lieutenant Edward Westfall, Fifth Coast Guard
    District Lighthouse Program Manager

Foreword.. P.3
    Robert Goodlatte, Representative
    Sixth District of Virginia
    United States Congress

Acknowledgements................................ P.5
Special Thanks.................................. P.6

The Lure of The Light........................... P.7

Location Map.................................... P.8

Introduction.................................... P.9

Assateague Lighthouse........................... P.11
Cape Charles Lighthouse......................... P.13
Cape Henry Lighthouse........................... P.15
New Cape Henry Lighthouse....................... P.17
Chesapeake Lighthouse........................... P.19
Lightship Portsmouth............................ P.21
Newport News Middle Ground Lighthouse........... P.23
Old Point Comfort Lighthouse.................... P.25
Thimble Shoals Lighthouse....................... P.27
New Point Comfort Lighthouse.................... P.29
Wolf Trap Lighthouse............................ P.31
Smith Point Lighthouse.......................... P.33
Jones Point Lighthouse.......................... P.35

Bibliography.................................... P.37
Index... P.38

About The Author................................ P.39

Appendix.. P.40
    Chronological Listing of Virginia's
        Lighthouses
    Information About the Photographers

Prologue

One aspect I hope you take with you from this book is how dynamic and creative the world of lighthouse program management is. Within the Fifth District, which includes Virginia, we have always worked hard, within our fiscal restraints, to reconcile the needs of the mariner. Additionally, we partner with state and local agencies and interested individuals and organizations to incorporate the American public's concern for these historic structures into the lighthouse program.

Since the middle of this century, the traditional functions of the lighthouse have been overtaken, to some extent, by improvements in navigational technology. Automation has changed the nature of the lighthouse itself. These changes have resulted in the removal of lighthouse keepers, the reduction to quarterly or semi-annual servicing, conversion to solar power, and finally, the removal from service (and sometimes demolition) of one-third of the Fifth District's lighthouses since about 1960.

Jerry's efforts to record and present these structures are most welcome. His changing impressions have been interesting to observe in the course of this project. A most gratifying realization is his appreciation of the efforts of our Aids to Navigation Teams (ANTs). The ANTs are the unsung foot soldiers in Coast Guard efforts to maintain aging structures in some of the harshest environments. These teams do what they do efficiently and with few people. At great cost to their personal schedules, they respond to outages that always seem to occur "after hours." The ANTs are responsible for lighthouses, buoys, fixed light structures and unlighted structures.

Several additional resources that help keep lighthouses in shape at low cost are our Buoy Tender crews, Coast Guard Reserve Lighthouse Maintenance Teams, and the Coast Guard Auxiliary. All work on specific lighthouse projects that help prolong more expensive commercial overhauls. Of particular note are the members of the Coast Guard Auxiliary, who perform this task, like all of their missions, as volunteers .

In closing, let me say that we are moving into an new phase of lighthouse program management. Shrinking budgets and improved technology require us to not only manage our resources better, but to engage partners beyond the Federal government. In the Fifth District, we have developed partnerships with museums, preservation groups, other government agencies, State Historic Preservation Offices and similar organizations. Our "partners" are taking an active role in sharing both the burdens and rewards of maintaining these symbols of America's Maritime History.   Enjoy!

Lieutenant Edward Westfall
Lighthouse Program Manager
Fifth Coast Guard District, Portsmouth, Virginia

Foreword

Virginia has only twelve lighthouses and one lightship remaining. Nine of these sentinels are still on the official "Coast Guard List" of active aids to navigation. Jones Point Lighthouse has recently been refurbished on the outside and illuminated. The lighthouse is now owned by the National Park Service, and serves as a private aid to navigation. New Point Comfort Lighthouse is now the property of Mathews County. Thanks to local authorities, there are extensive plans being formulated for the restoration and preservation of this noble and picturesque structure. Old Cape Henry Lighthouse has long abdicated its responsibility to its new counterpart, and is open as a tourist attraction. Lightship Portsmouth, now serving as a museum, has been beautifully restored, and lies in repose in dry dock. The remainder of the lighthouses in Virginia still serve as proud and undaunted servants to the mariners of our glorious and beautiful waterways.

To my knowledge, this book represents the first complete history of all lighthouses still standing in Virginia. The work embodies many hours of research and many miles of travel in an effort to include those lights that are often overlooked due to difficult accessibility or a lesser intent to be all-inclusive.

Each lighthouse is pictured in full color. Interior photographs of each lighthouse offer the reader an insight not typically available in other works. This book will provide the lighthouse enthusiast with informative reading, and will serve as a valuable reference for information about the lighthouses of Virginia. Those interested in photography will enjoy a colorful and exciting visual experience.

Virginia's shorelines and inland waterways are a valuable resource of our commonwealth and nation. Lighthouses have always played an important role in marking safe courses of travel for the many military, commercial, industrial, and recreational activities of our people. I am encouraged by the recent surge of interest in lighthouses. It would be a shame if we were to abandon these epic monuments and allow them to fall to ruin.

I feel confident *Lighthouses of Virginia* will cultivate new interest in the restoration and preservation of these delightful and impressive structures.

Congressman Robert Goodlatte
6th District of Virginia House of Representatives
United States Congress

ANT KENNEBEC (L. to R.)
BM1 John Singletary, FN Scott Higgins,
MK2 Woody Towler, SA Brian Satterfield,
(Audrey and Jim Murphy, United States
Coast Guard Auxiliary, Flotilla 63)

ANT MILFORD HAVEN (L. to R.)
SN Steve Hart, SN Edward Garnett,
BMC Mike Dorman, MK3 Jim Sheehan,
BM3 Eric Kennedy, FN Matt Lorh

United States Coast Guard Station
Group Hampton Roads, Portsmouth,
Virginia

United States Coast Guard Station
Hudgins, Virginia

Electricians' Shop
EM1 Chris Vargo (standing), (L. to R.) EM1 Jim Ross, EM2 Dana Poulsen, EM2 Eric Boehmer

United States Coast Guard Station Group Hampton Roads Engineering
Portsmouth, Virginia

Paul DeVita
United States Coast Guard Auxiliary
Flotilla 66

Acknowledgements

The Honorable Robert Goodlatte
United States Congress
6th District House of Representatives, Virginia

Commander John Gentile, United States Coast Guard
Congressional and Governmental Affairs Staff Washington, D.C.

Lieutenant Edward Westfall, Lighthouse Program Manager
Fifth Coast Guard District Portsmouth, Virginia

Chief Warrant Officer Dave Merrill,
United States Coast Guard Group Hampton Roads, Portsmouth, Virginia

ANT KENNEBEC
United States Coast Guard Group Hampton Roads, Portsmouth, Virginia
BM1 John Singletary (The guy that makes things happen!)
MK2 Woody Towler
FN Scott Higgins
SA Brian Satterfield

Electricians' Shop
United States Coast Guard Group Hampton Roads Engineering, Portsmouth, Virginia
EM1 Chris Vargo (The guy with quiet determination!)
EM1 Jim Ross (The guy with all the answers!)
EM2 Dana Poulsen
EM2 Eric Boehmer

ANT MILFORD HAVEN
United States Coast Guard Station Hudgins, Virginia
Chief Petty Officer Mike Dorman
BM3 Eric Kennedy (The guy with perseverance!)
BM1 Mike Von Engle
MK3 Jim Sheehan
SN Steve Hart
SN Edward Garnett
FN Matt Lorh

United States Coast Guard Station Cape Henry, Virginia
MK1 Chuck Gibson
Keeper, New Cape Henry Lighthouse

United States Coast Guard Auxiliary
Paul Devita, Flotilla 66
Audrey and Jim Murphy, Flotilla 63

George Washington Memorial Parkway
National Park Service
Creg Howland, Historian

Portsmouth Museums
Betty Burnell, Director
Alice Hanes, Curator, Lightship and Naval Shipyard Museums
Benjamin Ellis, Museum Curatorial Assistant, Lightship Museum
Karla Kirk, Interpreter, Lightship Museum
Michael Kerekesh, Curatorial Assistant II

Special Thanks

During the writing, photographing, and researching for this book, I was assisted by many members of the Fifth Coast Guard District, Group Hampton Roads, Portsmouth, Virginia and more specifically by the **ANTs,** who are responsible for the repair and maintenance of Virginia's lighthouses. Were it not for their assistance and ready cooperation, this work would not have been possible.

While making the many contacts with personnel responsible for certain lights, I was referred to individuals who would provide access to the lights and provide transportation by boat as necessary. Invariably, I was told, "He will help you. He's a nice guy." And, in fact, each was, indeed, "A nice guy!"

Transportation to each lighthouse was willingly and graciously provided, either by Coast Guard active personnel, or the Coast Guard Auxiliary. During my visits to the various lighthouses, I was first and foremost impressed by the reception from all personnel with whom I worked. Not once was I treated as if I was an imposition or a bother. The cordial, friendly demeanor of everyone was beyond expectations, and certainly above and beyond the call of duty.

It was a distinct privilege and a memorable experience to have shared the adventures I encountered with a group of such dedicated, professional, and energetic young men. During our many voyages, I was able to witness first hand the competent and professional manner in which these Guardsmen performed their duties. Whether searching for a sunken barge, setting a temporary warning light, taking under tow a stranded waterman, or arranging for an emergency evacuation of a sick passenger, these young sea farers conducted themselves as a well trained, efficient team in order to accomplish their task. Each task was done quickly and effectively with a high level of skill exhibiting the fruits of their exemplary training and dedication to their job.

Members of the United States Coast Guard **ANT Kennebec, ANT Milford Haven, ANT Chincoteague,** and **Flotilla 66 of the Coast Guard Auxiliary** were extremely helpful in providing the means to make this work a reality. I express my gratitude and appreciation for all their assistance.

From the onset of this project, **Representative Bob Goodlatte**, United States Congress, and **Lieutenant Ed Westfall**, Fifth Coast Guard District, were always very accommodating and offered every possible assistance in order for me to accomplish my goal. Thank you to these fine gentlemen!

The Lure Of The Light

A mystical experience unfolds when one stands watching a lighthouse just before dark, waiting for the quiet sentinel to awaken and exhibit its life-giving and energizing beam of light. The ever-rolling sea sings its majestic song, forever enduring. A warm and gentle summer breeze fingers through your hair, pushing your locks upward off your forehead, brushing your cheeks ever so gently. The call of a distant seagull floats softly to your ear. The moon and the stars join you and offer comfort and wait with you. They give peace and tranquility.

The beacon stands quiet and still, resting for its long vigil of the night. Then with regularity and without fail, the rays burst forth from the lantern room signaling:

"Now I am awake. Now I shine my light to fill and warm your heart...to guide and direct you...I serve you in all times. I lead you in safety to where your heart will take you. I will show you the way to where your heart longs to be, to where your dreams become real...to where you life is complete. I will never fail you, for I am your friend. I will be here always to give you the ray of hope that you need. I am here today, and I will be here tomorrow, for all your tomorrows and all the wonders they will bring you. Keep your faith as I faithfully shine my light for you. I am strong and steadfast and forever devoted to you...The Light of Love and Hope will forever shine!"

Evening silhouette of New Cape Henry Lighthouse

To
MOM and DAD
Jessie and Anthony Zaccaria
"The Light of Love and Hope will forever shine!"

LOCATION MAP

1. ASSATEAGUE
2. CAPE CHARLES
3. CHESAPEAKE
4. NEW CAPE HENRY
5. OLD CAPE HENRY
6. LIGHTSHIP PORTSMOUTH
7. NEWPORT NEWS MIDDLE GROUND
8. OLD POINT COMFORT
9. THIMBLE SHOALS
10. NEW POINT COMFORT
11. WOLF TRAP
12. SMITH POINT
13. JONES POINT

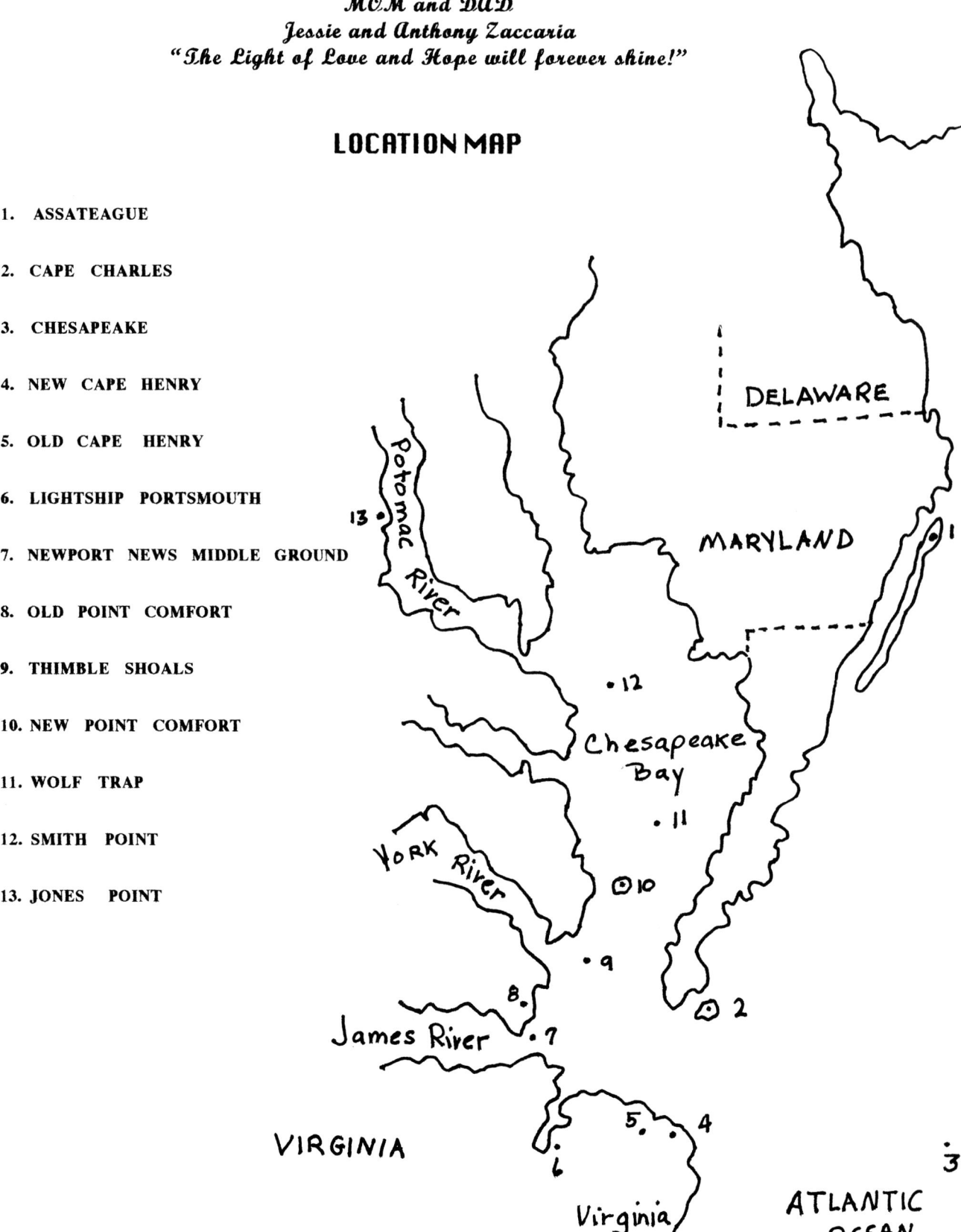

Introduction

Lighthouses possess a special charm and wonder that appeal to people from many walks of life. The fascination of the sea and all things associated with the glory and majesty of this mighty force gives us a sense of awe and amazement. The mission of the lighthouse is to deal with all the terrific forces of nature and its many mood swings and to stand strong and stalwart in the performance of its duty. Lighthouses are charged with the responsibility of marking a path of safe travel and a warning of the dangers that confront all those who travel our waterways. The lighthouse cannot fail to fulfill its mission, for the lives of mariners of all sorts depend upon it for guidance when conditions might be the worst for anyone sailing the vast expanses of the oceans, rivers, and lakes of the world.

The lighthouses in Virginia vary widely in style and structure. Three of Virginia's lighthouses are *octagonal* masonry towers, another is *conical.* One is a *skeletal* tower (a steel tower with supporting beams giving it a skeletal appearance), and two are *caissons* (metal tubs filled with concrete sitting on the bottom of the bay).

As with all lighthouses, each of Virginia's lights has its own personality portrayed through unique markings, its design, or its *characteristic* (the particular manner in which a lighthouse beacon shines or flashes). The characteristics vary in **duration** of flash, **pattern** of flash, and **color**. Each of these elements identifies the lighthouse and its location, distinguishing it from all other lighthouses.

The painted patterns of the towers serve as **day marks** which can be identified in clear weather. The alternating red and white stripes of the Assateague Island tower signal to the sailor that he is approaching the northern border of Virginia. The distinctive, alternating black and white panels of New Cape Henry Lighthouse signal the route to the haven and safety of the Chesapeake Bay.

Virginia's lighthouses are found on the shore, in the shallow waters of the Chesapeake Bay, and on picturesque deserted islands. One is located in the Atlantic Ocean, far off shore from the many important ports and harbors in Virginia. This lighthouse is not only unlike any other in the state, but is also one of a few of like design in the nation.

LIGHTHOUSES OF VIRGINIA will serve as a pictorial reference for those seeking information about the history, location, and style of all remaining lighthouses located on Virginia waterways. Information about the accessibility of the light, directions for locating the light, historical data, and architectural information will be given. Our pictorial tour of the lighthouses of Virginia will begin with the Assateague Island Lighthouse located near the northern tip of Virginia's Eastern Shore. We will then travel southward along the Virginia coastline, out into the openness of the Atlantic Ocean, northward up the Chesapeake Bay, and finally up the Potomac River, ending at the only remaining river lighthouse in Virginia.

Lighthouse enthusiasts, vacationers, history lovers, and those who enjoy photography will experience the first complete guide to all the remaining lighthouses in Virginia. During your lighthouse hunting, be sure to visit the interesting tourist attractions close by that will enhance your tour of our beautiful commonwealth.

Assateague Island Lighthouse (1867) is Virginia's only conical tower.

Impressive brick arches at the entrance foyer and around the window wells amplify Assateague's uncommon elegance.

Spiral staircase leading to the lantern room of Assateague Island Lighthouse

Assateague Island Lighthouse

The Assateague Lighthouse is one of the most beautiful lighthouses in Virginia. Its beauty is paralleled only by the colorful interior of New Cape Henry Lighthouse. The natural (unpainted) brick walls and floors give a warm comfortable feeling to visitors. The majestic brick arches at the entrance foyer and around the windows add a special charm peculiar only to the Assateague Lighthouse. The characteristic is one white flash every five seconds. A primary and secondary rotating aerobeacon have replaced the original lantern. If the primary light should go out, the secondary light would automatically ignite. A **Daylight Control Monitoring System** activates the light at dusk. The keeper's house sits just yards from the tower, and is occupied by National Park personnel.

For many years, darkness prevailed along the Virginia coastline with no beacons to warn of the many dangerous shoals to the north of Cape Charles. The growth in coastal trade, and the increasing number of shipwrecks along this strip mandated the construction of the first Assateague Lighthouse in 1833. The onset of the War Between the States interrupted plans for extending the height of the lighthouse. Finally, in **1867**, a new tower was erected. This brick conical tower stands at 142 feet, is 27 1/2 feet wide at the base, and is painted with distinctive, alternating red and white bands. It originally housed a first order Fresnel lens.[1]

A major nemesis to lighthouses is the erosion of the land. This act of nature has caused the demise of many lighthouses throughout history and continues to be a major threat to many of the remaining sentinels. At one time, the Assateague Lighthouse stood near the edge of the island's shore. However, converse to what is happening to the sites of many lighthouses, Assateague Island has, over the years, been built up by the same forces that threaten to wear away many locations where these beacons of hope stand. The Tom's Grove Hook (the southern tip of Assateague Island) is slowly being extended by currents along the shoreline (**littoral currents**) that are depositing huge quantities of sand to the lower tip of the island. The major portion of this "hook" did not exist during the late 1800s. It is anticipated that this hook will eventually close itself up and form a lagoon at the end of the island. Unlike many islands, Assateague is growing larger each year.

Assateague Island is open to visitors from 6:00 A.M. to 8:00 P.M. The island offers not only the opportunity to visit the lighthouse, but also the chance to observe the many and varied species of wildlife including native White Tailed Deer and a smaller species of elk (Sika Elk), a variety of ducks and other waterfowl, and, of course, the famous wild ponies that graze and live in the marshlands of the island. Woodland trails and bicycle paths are available for visitors to make the most of this nature haven. At the southern end of Assateague Island is a beautiful, uncluttered beach area with bath facilities. Guided marsh walks, bird walks, and beach walks are offered by the Rangers at the Tom's Grove Visitors' Center from 9:00 A.M. until 4:00 P.M. daily. An entrance fee of $4 for the vehicle and all passengers is collected at the toll gate at the entrance to Assateague Island, and a visitors' pass is issued that is valid for 7 days.

Chincoteague Island offers an abundance of overnight accommodations in a quaint and moderately commercialized setting. The merchants and shop owners are friendly, and you will receive a wholesome, hometown welcome. Also worthy of visiting while on Chincoteague Island is the Oyster and Maritime Museum.

From Route 13 on the eastern shore, take Route 175 onto Chincoteague Road to Chincoteague Island. Cross the bridge; turn left on Main Street. Turn right onto Maddox Boulevard; continue to travel southward to Assateague Island. The lighthouse can be seen towering over the pine trees off to the right just as you cross the bridge entering the Chincoteague National Wildlife Refuge. It is located in the Assateague National Seashore Park that encompasses the entire island. The parking lot is one quarter of a mile from the entrance gate on the right side of the road. Assateague Island Lighthouse is a quarter of a mile down Lighthouse Trail.

Assateague Lighthouse was repainted in 1994, is structurally sound, and is in excellent condition. The tower and grounds are easily accessible. However, the lighthouse is still operating and is only open for special group tours arranged through ANT Chincoteague.

---

[1] Bruce Roberts and Ray Jones, *Southern Lighthouses* (Old Saybrook, Connecticut: The Globe Pequot Press, 1995) 18.

Cape Charles Lighthouse, located on Smith Island (1895), is Virginia's only skeletal tower.

Spiral stairs leading to the lantern room of Cape Charles Lighthouse

Cape Charles Lighthouse

Cape Charles Lighthouse differs in style and structure from other lighthouses found in Virginia. The design offers less resistance to wind and is, therefore, more often used in those areas that suffer frequent and violent hurricanes. However, it was not until several lighthouses were built on Smith Island that the structure evolved into the *skeletal tower* that is located there today.

The first light on Smith Island was a brick tower 55 feet tall, built in 1828. The foundation for the original light is now half a mile off the beach of the island and under the ocean. Because of the well substantiated complaints about this light, a replacement tower was approved. By 1864, the replacement light was in service and stood at 150 feet.[2]

The Cape Charles Lighthouse eventually became threatened by natural forces. The shoreline of Smith Island was eroding rapidly. At one time, the immediate site of the light station became an island, barely surviving the destruction of the surrounding waters. Attempts were made to provide protection from the encroaching waters. However, these efforts were unsuccessful, and it was decided that the light should be replaced and relocated.[3]

After 3 years of construction, in **1895**, a third lighthouse stood on Smith Island. This steel tower stands at the height of 191 feet. It was originally fitted with a first order Fresnel lens. The tower is painted white, with the watch room and lantern room painted black. It is supported by eight massive iron "legs" that run the length of the tower. In 1963, the Fresnel lens was removed, the light was automated, and the lens was replaced with airport beacons. The Cape Charles Light has now been fitted with a modern lantern. The focal point of the lamp is 180 feet from the base of the tower. The lantern is illuminated by six two-volt batteries that are charged by six 43-watt solar panels facing south. The lantern room is enclosed by 48 rectangular panels of glass and is 18 feet tall. It now houses a new type lantern the Coast Guard is using called the VRB-25 (**Vega Rotating Beacon** nicknamed **VEGA lantern**). The 50-watt, 12-volt D.C. lantern is capable of illumination up to 20 miles. The lantern emits a white flash every 5 seconds 30 minutes before sunset until 30 minutes after sunrise.[4]

The lighthouse sits on the western side of Smith Island. The central iron "tube" contains the spiral staircase that leads to the lantern room. The diameter of the tube is only 12 feet. Two hundred-sixteen steps bring you to the generator room where the electronic equipment is located. This room has wood floors and walls, painted gray, and 3 windows facing north. Seventeen steps more lead to the watch room with metal floors, walls, and ceiling. At this level, the lower gallery is accessible through the full-size metal door. The gallery has a solid metal floor and two-inch pipe railing.

The old antenna for the **A.M.C.S.** (Automated Monitoring Control System) is located on the lower gallery. At one time, the antenna at Cape Charles shot a signal to a similar antenna on the Cape Henry Lighthouse to monitor the operation of all equipment at the light, which, in turn, could be controlled by the Coast Guard Station Group Hampton Roads in Portsmouth. The antenna is now non-functional, and is scheduled to be dismantled.

The light station consists of the tower, the keeper's house, a frame storage building behind the house, and two brick storage houses located behind the tower. The large and impressive keeper's house sits, forlorn and abandoned, with its windows and doors boarded up. The exterior of the house is in very good repair, needing only minor attention. However, the interior of the house is in need of total renovation. Plaster has fallen from the walls and ceilings, and rubble is found in every room. At one time, the house was quite adequate for the keeper and a large family. The first floor has a kitchen, dining room, parlor, study, pantry, and bathroom. The winding staircase leads to the second floor, which has six bedrooms and a stairway to the attic.

From the Virginia Beach area, cross the Chesapeake Bay Bridge-Tunnel. There is a toll for the car and all passengers. Upon exiting the tunnel, you arrive on Fisherman Island on the Eastern Shore of Virginia. Route 13 North will take you to Lankford Road, where you turn right onto Seaside Road; then to Fitchetts Road at the entrance to Eastern Shore of Virginia National Wildlife Refuge. Continue to Wise Point, where you may launch your boat at the public boat ramp. There is a $10.00 fee for use of the boat ramp. The boat must have a shallow draft in order to maneuver around and between the sand bars located in **Magothy Bay**. One must be knowledgeable of the comings and goings of the tides in order to make this trip successfully. After a pleasant, ten minute boat ride, you arrive at Smith Island, where the lighthouse is located. In order to land on the island, one must navigate the shallow waters and locate a sand barge on which to travel by foot for about a half-mile using hip waders to approach the island. Even for the Coast Guard, the approach to the island is a trial and error mission. The depth of the water is a determinant to the approach. If the water is too deep, you must get back on board, locate shallow waters that will not top your waders and try again. The boat will have to be towed by hand the remainder of the trip. Upon landing, follow the foot path through the waist-high, tick-infested marsh grass for about a quarter of a mile. Smith Island is approximately one mile long and one-half mile wide. When visiting the lighthouse, bring plenty of tick and mosquito spray. Depending on the time of the year, if the ticks are not in abundance, the mosquitoes surely will be. The Tiger Mosquitoes are 3 times the size of fresh water mosquitoes and very aggressive. The infestation is worst between April and October. Visitation is advisable during the late Fall or early Spring.

With the exception of needing exterior painting, the tower is in good condition and still operating. It is not open to the public.

Cape Henry Lighthouse still stands although it was expected to fall to ruins years ago.

Cape Henry lighthouse was constructed of sandstone. The interior was lined with brick in 1857.

---

[2] F. Ross Holland, Jr., *America's Lighthouses* (Mineola, New York: Dover Publications, 1988) 122.
[3] Holland, *America's Lighthouses*, 122.
[4] Holland, *America's Lighthouses*, 122.

Cape Henry Lighthouse

Rarely is one fortunate enough to have the chance to visit two lighthouses at one location. The original Cape Henry Lighthouse is located on a small knoll just a few hundred feet from its replacement tower. Other buildings have long been destroyed, and only the octagonal sandstone tower remains. At the foot of the path leading up to the tower is a small visitor's booth. Literature about the lighthouse can be obtained from one of the assistants working in the small information house.

Visitors may climb to the top of the 90 foot lighthouse and enter the lantern room through a small opening in the floor that was meant only to be entered by people of slender stature. The lens originally located in the **bird-cage style** lantern room has been removed. Visitors may look directly east into the lantern room of the New Cape Henry Lighthouse as well as enjoy the panoramic view of the Virginia Beach coastline.

In 1789, construction of the Cape Henry Lighthouse was begun, and by **1792** the tower was completed. This was the first lighthouse to be authorized and built by the newly-formed Federal Government, during the presidency of George Washington. In 1857, the lighthouse was reinforced with a brick lining and fitted with a Fresnel lens. The Cape Henry Lighthouse was no less a target for Confederate troops than many other lighthouses during the Civil War. In the early 1860s, the lighthouse fell subject to raids by Confederate troops trying to darken the southern coastline for protection from Federal invaders. The Confederates destroyed the lens, and the light was dark until 1863, when the lens was replaced. By the 1870s, apparent signs of serious faults in the walls of the tower, became a source of concern, and it was expected to be destroyed by any storm of considerable strength. For this reason, construction of a new lighthouse was deemed necessary. However, the old tower still stands today.[5]

The lighthouse is open for visits from March 15 until the end of October. A two dollar entrance fee is charged. The lighthouse, with its new counterpart, is located inside the perimeter of Fort Story Military Base. Entrance to the fort is available from 5:00 A.M. until 11:00 P.M. A ten-minute drive from the heart of the resort area of Virginia Beach will bring you to the lighthouses. Travel north on Atlantic Avenue to 89th street to the entrance to Fort Story. Watch for a sharp right turn and continue past the guard station until you reach Cape Henry Road. Parking is readily available in front of both lighthouses. Cape Henry Lighthouse is open for visitors from 10:00 A.M. until 5:00 P.M. The lighthouse has been the property of the Association for the Preservation of Virginia Antiquities since 1930. For information, contact the Association at (804) 648-1889 or call the Cape Henry Lighthouse at (757) 422-9421.

Windows and storage bins are recessed in the brick liner of the interior.

[5] F. Ross Holland, Jr., *Great American Lighthouses* (Washington, D.C.: The Preservation Press, 1995) 162-63.

New Cape Henry Lighthouse (1879) stands majestically watching over the entrance to the Chesapeake Bay.

The beautifully painted staircase is one of the most attractive features of New Cape Henry Lighthouse.

16 The entrance level at New Cape Henry Lighthouse

New Cape Henry Lighthouse

The New Cape Henry Lighthouse is, without question, the most beautiful and stately lighthouse in Virginia. The tower has been repainted inside and out and is in the best condition of any lighthouse in the state. It typifies the complete light station of the past, with its three keeper's dwellings, well-kept and attractively landscaped grounds, and associated service buildings.

Construction began in 1879, and was completed in **1881**. The new cast iron octagonal tower was placed within yards of the site of the old Cape Henry Tower, and closer to the shore. It was originally illuminated by oil lamps and Argand reflectors. The lantern was fitted with a first order Fresnel lens that was built in Paris in 1880. The original lens still remains in place. The light was converted to electricity in 1923. A secondary lamp automatically ratchets into position if the primary lamp burns out. If total power is lost, an automatic generator provides back-up power for the station.

The navigational significance of New Cape Henry Light Station has changed over the years. It is not generally known that there is a full-time keeper who lives on the station, overseeing its daily operation and maintaining the light and other sophisticated electronic equipment. The principal reason this is still a manned light station is the **Global Positioning System (GPS)** located at the site. This is a system that relays information from a cluster of satellites allowing ships' captains to pin-point their exact location within a margin of error of a few feet. Should this system "go down" for any reason, it is the keeper's responsibility to reactivate it with all expediency. Cape Henry is the only GPS site on the East Coast that is accompanied by an active light station.

This superb and majestic structure towers over the waters of Cape Henry at the southern entrance to the Chesapeake Bay, guiding sea-going vessels safely around the Cape as they make their way into the inland waterways. The tower stands 163 feet tall. The 1,000-watt electric light bulb flashes a white signal. Its *characteristic*, . . _ (dot, dot, dash), represents the letter "U" in Morse code. There is also a red sector that warns captains of the presence of dangerous shoal areas. The cast iron panels are alternately painted black and white. The tower has a masonry lining. The interior of the light tower is impressively and attractively painted with bright colors that give it its special charm and beauty. The tile mosaic floor at the base of the tower is a most unusual and attractive feature. The excellent state of repair of New Cape Henry Lighthouse is a credit to the outstanding efforts of personnel at U.S. Coast Guard Group Hampton Roads Engineering. The exterior of the tower was scraped and repainted in 1994. The three remaining dwellings are occupied by Coast Guard personnel. The Keeper lives in "B Quarters" (the center house).

The lighthouse is located only a few minutes drive north from Virginia Beach resort area, in the boundaries of Fort Story Military Base at the U.S. Coast Guard Station, Cape Henry. At the entrance to the base, an armed guard will stop travelers and ask for driver's license identification and the intent of the visitor. Simply state, " I wish to visit the lighthouses." Passage will be granted until the base closes to the public each evening.

Vacationers may enjoy watching the flash of the lighthouse while having a romantic, candlelight dinner in one of the roof-top restaurants located along the shores of northern Virginia Beach.

The light and station are still active and not open to the public. However, one may view the tower and the dwellings of the light station from just yards away, outside the wood fence that surrounds the site.

The tower, fog signals, and solar panels are located on the flight deck of Chesapeake Lighthouse.

The VEGA lantern located in the Chesapeake Lighthouse

Chesapeake Lighthouse (1965) has all the amenities for comfortable, extended visits.

Chesapeake Lighthouse

The architecture of Chesapeake Lighthouse is one of the most unique in the country. It is not at all what we think of when considering lighthouses. It more closely resembles an off-shore oil rig. The ***Texas Tower*** is the most recent and modern structure designed and built in this country for use as an aid to navigation.

Chesapeake Lighthouse was built in **1965**, thirteen miles off shore from Cape Henry, in 38 feet of water. It replaced Lightship Chesapeake, which is now a museum ship located at Inner Harbor in Baltimore. Its characteristic is two white flashes, with a 15-second interval of darkness. The maintenance deck is 60 feet above the water. The living quarters are 80 feet above the water line, and the flight deck (helipad) is 90 feet high. The focal point of the lens is 120 feet above the sea. Chesapeake Lighthouse is a massive structure dominating the lonely and isolated span of ocean off the coast of Virginia Beach. The living quarters consists of seven dormitory-style bedrooms, each containing its own chest of drawers and locker space. The generator room containing the electronic equipment and power sources occupies approximately one fourth of the interior. There is a fully-equipped galley and a large recreation room containing a television, stereo, pool table, and comfortable furniture. The lighthouse can adequately accommodate extended visits for as many as 14 people. Power for the **Vega** lantern (identical to the one on Cape Charles Lighthouse) and the two fog signals, stacked one on top of the other on the flight deck, is provided by six 2-volt batteries that are charged by sixteen 2 1/2 square feet solar panels also located on the flight deck. The light is visible for 20 miles. The fog signal emits a 3-second blast followed by a 27-second interval of silence. It is audible for 1/2 mile. Due to the lack of regular use and maintenance, the interior of the lighthouse shows some signs of neglect. But, in general, the structure is in good repair. On a very clear day, the Chesapeake Lighthouse can be seen from the tower of New Cape Henry.

There are three identical Texas Towers in the Fifth District Lighthouse Program. **Diamond Shoals** is located 12 miles off shore from Cape Hatteras, North Carolina and **Frying Pan Shoals** is located 30 miles out from Cape Lookout, North Carolina. All three Texas Towers in the Fifth District are solarized and serviced once every three months. While the exteriors and lighting apparatuses are maintained regularly, the interiors receive no attention. This is due to the fact that they are no longer manned and the return for the investment is not evident due to the lack of use.

The **Ambrose Lighthouse** replaced Ambrose Lightship (LV 87) in 1967, and is located off the eastern shore of Long Island, New York. (Texas Towers typically were built to replace lightships.) It was crashed into by a ship, causing the emergency replacement of one of the legs. The Texas tower at **Buzzard's Bay, Massachusetts** has been decommissioned and dismantled. The tower at **Savannah, Georgia** was rammed by a large sailing vessel and totally destroyed in 1996. Texas Towers are built in the most exposed and isolated locations, and are susceptible to damage from collision as well as storms and hurricanes. All of the Texas Towers were designed identically, each containing a landing pad for helicopters. Each also had a boat landing. These have all been destroyed, and approach is most often made by helicopter. These lighthouses were manned by Coast Guard personnel until the late 1970s and early 1980s when they were automated. Duty on the secluded lighthouses was usually served in 7-10 day tours followed by off duty time of the same length.

Like many other lighthouses, the Texas Towers are diminishing in value as aids to navigation, and the Coast Guard is searching for other agencies to take them over. The immediate future of Chesapeake Lighthouse is uncertain because it is expensive to operate and maintain. It is also expensive to dismantle these structures. The Coast Guard is talking with the Navy with hopes of transferring ownership of the Chesapeake Light over to them. Universities have also indicated some interest in the structure for research and development programs. Chesapeake Lighthouse is scheduled to be decommissioned in the year 2004.

Chesapeake Lighthouse is still operating and is not open to the public. It is reached only by boat or helicopter traveling directly east off Cape Henry.

Lightship Portsmouth (1916) has been the victim of many collisions by other vessels.

The storm helm aboard LV 101

The original Fresnel lens from Smith Point Lighthouse is on display in the Lightship Museum.

20

Lightship Portsmouth (LV 101)

Virginia is one of the few states fortunate enough to provide the final resting place for a most unusual aid to navigation, the **Lightship.** LV 101 is one of only 14 lightships still in existence in this country. The first lightship was stationed at Craney Island in Portsmouth, in 1820. The last lightship was decommissioned in 1985. During this time, a total of 120 light vessels were in service.

Lightships were used to mark waters where it was too perilous or too costly to construct a typical lighthouse, where a temporary light was needed during repairs to a lighthouse, or as an interim light during construction of more permanent light stations.

While not the typical lighthouse, the lightship served an identical purpose. The lifestyle afforded on a lightship was even more spartan than that of the typical lighthouse keeper, and the dangers even greater due to the often isolated and exposed locations. In 1934, The **Olympia, (the Titanic's sister ship)** rammed a lightship, cutting the vessel in half. During her tenure of service, LV 101 was the target of 24 different collisions with other ships. On eight occasions, she was rammed by other vessels while serving at Cape Charles. Most of the collisions were glancing blows and caused minor damage. An examination of the exterior of the ship's hull will reveal indentations caused by these unexpected encounters.

LV 101 was powered by a 4 cylinder kerosene engine when she embarked on her maiden voyage to serve as **Lightship Charles** (Cape Charles) on September 18, **1916.** She also served at sites in Delaware, Maryland, and Massachusetts. In 1944, she was fitted with a new 6 cylinder, 350 hp Cooper-Bessemer engine. The vessel was capable of traveling at a top speed of 8.2 knots. Lightship Portsmouth is 100 feet 10 inches in length. Her lantern perches on a single mast that rises from the center of the radio room. The flash characteristic is a white light signaling ._. (dot, dash, dot...the letter P in Morse code), with a 15-second interval of darkness. The vessel was one of only two steel, **Whale-Back** (round-hulled) lightships ever built. The other was her sister ship, LV 102. The Lightship was decommissioned in 1964. In 1967, she was donated to the city of Portsmouth, and was retired to the status of a museum ship. LV 101 now rests dry-docked in a huge concrete slab.

Several beautiful lighthouse lenses are displayed on the main deck of the Lightship Museum. The original 3 1/2 order Fresnel lens removed from Smith Point Lighthouse is brilliantly showcased at the entrance. The lens cost $2,500 when it was made in 1894. In 1970, several of the glass reflectors were vandalized. Nevertheless, the beauty of this valuable, nautical artifact has not diminished. The main deck houses the crew's quarters, Officers' quarters, the ships galley, and the enlisted men's mess. The Captain's cabin has a single bed, desk, porcelain sink, and closet. A nautical map is spread out open on the desk and the Captain's coat and hat lie on the bed, awaiting his return. Above the main deck is the Pilot House, radio room, and **storm helm** (a 4 1/2 feet brass ship's wheel). Most of the piloting of the ship was done from the **Flying Bridge** (the top deck), where there is another helm similar to the one below. On this deck, there are two lifeboats off each side, a fog horn, and two 3 1/2 feet air scoops that were the only source of fresh air for the crew. Hanging from the starboard side of the bow is the ship's auxiliary, 5,000 pound **mushroom anchor.** The mast has a brass bell attached that reads, "USLHS 1915." (United States Lighthouse Service, and the year in which the bell was cast). The lightship has been beautifully restored and appears "ready for service."

Traveling south on I-95, at Richmond exit on I-64 toward Norfolk/Virginia Beach. Just before the Hampton Roads Tunnel, take I-664 South to the Monitor-Merrimac Bridge Tunnel. Take Route 164 East to Portsmouth. Turn right on Mount Vernon Avenue and continue to London Boulevard. Turn left onto London Boulevard and continue to Water Street. The Lightship Museum is located on Water Street where London ends. It is open yearlong from 10:00 A.M. until 5:00 P.M., Tuesday through Saturday, and from 1:00 P.M. until 5:00 P.M. on Sundays. Only the main deck is open to the public.

While visiting Lightship Portsmouth, you should definitely take the time to visit the Arts Center, The Children's Museum, and the Naval Shipyard Museum, all located within a short walking distance from the Lightship. For information contact the offices of Portsmouth Museums at 757-393-8393.

The Olde Towne Historic District, the Dismal Swamp Tour, The Virginia Sports Hall of Fame, the Olde Towne Trolley Tour, Hill House, and many other attractions are available for your touring pleasure. For more information contact the Portsmouth Convention and Visitors Bureau at 1-800-PORTS-VA or 757-393-5111.

Newport News Middle Ground Lighthouse
(1891)

Looking out to the gallery from the
watch room of Middle Ground Lighthouse

Newport News Middle Ground Lighthouse

This cast iron **caisson** sits on a shoal located at Hampton Roads. The structure was erected in **1891**, and was painted brown. It sits in 15 feet of water, the average depth of the Chesapeake Bay. The 52 feet high lighthouse has four stories below the lantern room. A fog bell tolls 24 hours a day 10 months out of the year. This is the **oldest caisson lighthouse remaining in Virginia.** It was automated in 1954. Its characteristic is a white flash every 6 seconds. The lighthouse sits in an important location marking the busy Newport News Channel, guiding large ships to the entrance to the James River.[6]

Middle Ground is now solar powered. The panels charge two 12-volt batteries that sit on the floor in the lantern room. The lens has been removed and the illumination is provided by a small lamp rising from an exterior pole above the gallery.

The iron entrance ladder hangs from the lower deck of the lighthouse and leads to a hatch in the floor of the deck. The ladder reverts itself, making it necessary to swing around to the backside of the ladder after climbing the first 10 feet section. This provides a real challenge in rough weather.

The five levels of the caisson structure, the basement, main floor, equipment room, watch room, and the the lantern room all have various shaped windows. The round, square, and rectangular windows have all been boarded over.

The basement has large block and brick walls with a concrete floor, presenting a dungeon-like appearance. A central iron pole runs up the height of the lighthouse, giving support to the floors above.

On the main floor, the walls are brick-lined 3/4 of the way around the semicircular rooms, with the remainder made of wood. The floor is made of unpainted tongue and groove boards.

The watch room above has tongue and groove wooden walls with an iron floor. The octagonal lantern room is accessed by way of an iron ladder leading up to a 3'x 3' hatch opening in the ceiling of the watch room below. The original glass panes have been removed and replaced with plexiglass, which is now frosted over due to age and allows for poor visibility.

Middle Ground Lighthouse is in excellent repair. The exterior was scraped and painted red by Coast Guard personnel in June of 1997. A complete service inspection was conducted, but little was done to the interior.

The light is still active. Because of its location, it is accessible only by boat. It is not open to the public.

The basement of Middle Ground Lighthouse showing the block walls that line the caisson structure, just above water level

[6] Robert de Gast, *The Lighthouses of the Chesapeake* (Baltimore, Maryland: The Johns Hopkins University Press, 1973) 19.

Old Point Comfort Lighthouse (1802)

The round "knobs" on the stone steps in Old Point Comfort form a central column resembling the support posts of many metal spiral staircases.

Old Point Comfort Lighthouse

This quaint little tower of only 54 feet is octagonal in shape, and is made of stone and masonry material. The spiral staircase is made of hand-cut stone, stacked strategically one upon the other, and leads to the lantern room. The dome of the lantern room is red and the exterior trim is now painted a bright "loud" green. The tower is painted white. The lantern shines its red light across the mouth of the James River, where it empties into the Chesapeake Bay. The two-story keeper's house sits within feet of the light tower. The grounds are attractively landscaped, and the tower and dwelling are in an excellent state of repair. The 3 1/2 order Fresnel lens refracts and reflects the light from the 1,000 watt electric light bulb now located in the lantern.

This **second oldest lighthouse in Virginia**, located on the Chesapeake, was built in **1802**. For a short period of time, the lighthouse was occupied by the British during the War of 1812 and used as a watch post. The famous Civil War battle of the iron-clad vessels, the U.S.S. Monitor and the C.S.S Virginia, took place within sight of the Old Point Comfort lighthouse at Hampton Roads. The tower stands proudly shinning its beacon as it has since the early 1800s. From the Coast Guard dock looking eastward, Thimble Shoal Lighthouse is visible. [7]

A convenient and definitely worthwhile side trip is a visit to the Casemate Museum, located directly behind the lighthouse at Fort Monroe. Robert E. Lee, Lieutenant of Engineers, was instrumental in the construction of the fortress, which was completed in 1834. Fort Monroe was one of few Union Military posts that was not captured by the Confederates during the Civil War. Consequently, the lighthouse was undisturbed. At the conclusion of the war, Confederate President Jefferson Davis was imprisoned at Fort Monroe in a barren and sparsely furnished **casemate** (a room used to house artillery, living quarters, or other equipment), where he was shackled with ankle irons upon his arrival. Edgar Allan Poe, Sergeant Major of Artillery, served at Fort Monroe in 1828. The self-guided, walking tour of the Casement Museum offers the opportunity to view the imprisonment casement of Jefferson Davis, a variety of artillery weapons, narrative videos and a small souvenir shop. The museum is open from 10:30 A.M. to 4:30 P.M. daily. It is closed only on Thanksgiving, Christmas, and New Year's Day. Admission is free. For information call (804) 727-3391 or write to Casemate Museum, P.O. Box 341, Fort Monroe, Virginia 23651.

Easy access to Old Point Comfort Lighthouse is gained from Interstate 64 traveling eastward. Turn left just before entering the Hampton Roads Tunnel at exit 268 onto Route 169, which is South Mallory Street. Turn right onto Route 143 East, which is East Mellen Street. Stop at the guard house at the entrance to Fort Monroe. Proceed to Officers Row and turn left. The lighthouse is located approximately one quarter of a mile from the old and once very exclusive Chamberlain Hotel. The setting is beautiful and offers wonderful opportunities for photographs of this scenic and attractive little lighthouse. Parking space is available at the sea wall located just across the street.

Old Point Comfort is still in use, and not open to the public, but you may walk right up to the tower and tour the grounds.

Evidence of moisture invasion in the upper portion of the Old Point Comfort tower

Thimble Shoals Lighthouse (1914)

The very narrow staircase is located in the entrance foyer at the main deck level of Thimble Shoals Lighthouse.

An interesting array of diamond and triangular shaped storm panes gives Thimble Shoal's lantern room its distinctive appearance.

Thimble Shoals Lighthouse

The first lighthouse was erected at Thimble Shoals in 1872. This hexagonal, **screwpile** structure stood only for a short time before a series of devastating mishaps began to plague it. The cause of the fire that destroyed the lighthouse in 1880 was never established. Because of its important location in the bay waters of Hampton Roads, the sentinel was replaced in less than two months. For the new screwpile, the series of ill-fated events continued. In the following years, the lighthouse was the victim of collisions with coal barges, steamers, and finally a schooner that rammed the structure causing it to catch fire and burn down. Remnants of the foundation still remain, protruding above water level near the present structure. Five years later, a new four-storied, cast-iron lighthouse was completed (in **1914**) on a **caisson foundation.** Thimble Shoals Lighthouse stands at 55 feet, the same height as Newport News Middle Ground Lighthouse. The characteristic is a white flash every 2.5 seconds. Automated in 1964, the need for a full-time keeper was eliminated. Thimble Shoals Lighthouse is located in the Chesapeake Bay, just outside the mouth of the Elizabeth River. The light is only a five minute boat ride eastward from Old Point Comfort Lighthouse.[8]

Entrance to Thimble Shoals Lighthouse is also tricky business. A straight metal ladder hangs from the side of the caisson and leads up through a 2 feet square trap door in the lower deck. There are no bumpers for the boat to rest against and the captain must be highly skilled in maneuvering and controlling the boat as visitors lunge from the bow onto the small ladder.

The lower deck is six feet wide with two rows of iron chains for railings. The main floor consists of a 5'x 8' entrance foyer and two semicircular rooms. Each room contains two porthole-style windows. The interior walls are made of steel. The outside walls are plaster, enclosed by the metal that surrounds the caisson. The concrete floor is covered with sheet linoleum that is cracking and peeling. The ceiling is made of iron.

A central column of steel supports the steps leading to the other floors, and runs from the basement to the third floor. The second floor also has two semi-circular rooms with all the walls made of metal. This gives the impression of being in a large metal tub (which, in fact, is true). When one pounds on the walls, the deep, rumbling, thunder-like sound of vibrating metal fills the room.

The narrow spiral staircase leads to the third floor, which also has two semi-circular rooms and porthole windows. An interesting feature is the bulges in the metal walls that have been caused by strong winds pounding against the lighthouse.

The lantern room is six feet in diameter, and is enclosed by triangular and diamond-shaped glass panes. There is a three square feet iron hatch door leading to the gallery where four 35-watt solar panels are located.

In 1996, the Thimble Shoals Lighthouse was sandblasted and repainted by the Coast Guard buoy tender, Red Cedar, that operates out of Coast Guard Station Group Hampton Roads, and is in an excellent state of repair. Again, only cosmetic work needs to be done to the interior, and the structure is generally in good repair.

The lighthouse is only accessible by boat. It is still in operation, and it is not open to the public.

---

[7] Roberts and Jones, *Mid-Atlantic Lighthouses* (Old Saybrook, Connecticut: The Globe Pequot Press, 1996) 77.

[8] de Gast, 31.

New Point Comfort
Lighthouse (1805)

The interior of New Point Comfort Lighthouse is
identical to Old Point Comfort.

New Point Comfort suffers the common problem of
moisture invasion at the upper portion of the tower.

New Point Comfort Lighthouse

New Point Comfort Lighthouse is the third **octagonal tower** to be built in Virginia. The sandstone tower is the second and last lighthouse still remaining in Virginia approved during the Presidency of Thomas Jefferson. It was built in **1805.** The tower was modeled after Old Point Comfort Lighthouse, and is 63 feet in height. These sister towers not only share the same design, but also share the common problem of interior moisture collection, causing the walls to be covered with mildew.

The lantern room was fitted with a fourth order lens typical of bay lights. Access to the lantern room is gained by ascending the unpainted limestone steps that are identical to the steps in Old Point Comfort Lighthouse. The light was originally fueled with whale oil; then kerosene; and later, acetylene. The fixed white light beaming at the entrance to Mobjack Bay was visible for 13 miles. The lantern room is enclosed by eleven trapezoidal panes of plexiglass, that have replaced the original glass panes.

In 1852, a sea captain, who had lain aside his sea-going days, served as the light keeper. He was assisted in the performance of his chores by a female slave. She was neither recognized nor compensated by the Lighthouse Board due to her "slave status." [9]

The beacon at New Point Comfort Lighthouse was also darkened by the Confederates during the Civil War, but was repaired and fitted with a new lens at the end of the war. The lens has since been removed, and only the iron pedestal that once supported the lens remains. The gallery is accessed by way of a 2'x 4' iron door at floor level of the lantern room. The dome is made of black iron. [10]

The island on which the lighthouse is located was actually once a point of land extending from the shore. However, a considerable storm severed the point from the mainland and formed a small island. The shell-covered island has now been eroded to an area approximately 100 feet in diameter, surrounded by rock rip rap to ward off further erosion. The station originally had a two story, frame, keeper's dwelling, but it was dismantled in 1919. No full-time keeper has served the lighthouse since that time. All that remains of the light station is the tower, which is in bad need of paint, although it is structurally sound. The light has not been functional for the past forty years. [11]

New Point Comfort Lighthouse is now the property of Mathews County, located where Route 14 ends. In April of 1997, hoping to spearhead a movement to increase public concern for this historic structure, Trenton Funkhouser, Director of Planning and Zoning for Mathews County and Paul DeVita, U.S. Coast Guard Auxiliary Commander, Flotilla 66, along with several members of the press, conducted a preliminary study to determine the needs for maintenance and repair of the lighthouse. Future plans include allocation of funds for needed repairs, regularly scheduled inspections and surveillance by Coast Guard personnel, the setting of an interpretive marker near the site, and a 200 linear feet boardwalk and observation deck that will allow visitors to view the lighthouse from shore. Due to this groundswell of local interest, the future of New Point Comfort Lighthouse looks very favorable. The lighthouse, accessible only by boat, is not open to the public. It is no longer operating.

---

[9] Holland, *Great American Lighthouses*, 160.
[10] de Gast, 35.
[11] de Gast, 35.

Wolf Trap Lighthouse (1894)

Stairway leading to the second floor of Wolf Trap

30

Wolf Trap Lighthouse

In 1691, the H.M.S. Wolfe struck a shoal located in the Chesapeake Bay. She was stranded on this shoal for ninety days. Because of this noteworthy mishap, the shoal was labeled "**Wolf Trap**". In 1821, a lightship was stationed at Wolf Trap Shoal to warn approaching vessels of its dangers. In 1861, Confederates attacked and sunk this lightship.[12]

It was not until several years after the Civil War, in 1870, that the lightship was replaced. This structure was intended to be a more permanent marker of this hazardous shoal. A hexagonal screwpile lighthouse was erected on this site, and remained in service until 1893, when it was torn off its foundation by an ice flow and was drifted down the bay. Again, a lightship was placed on the shoal to serve until another new structure was built in **1894.** The octagonal, red brick keeper's quarters was constructed on a **caisson** foundation and remains in place to this day. It was the **first of this type structure to be placed on a caisson foundation in Virginia**. From a height of 52 feet, the lantern emits a white flash every 15 seconds. Three 35- watt solar panels now charge the 12-volt batteries that provide energy for the lamp. Routine maintenance is required only once yearly at an average cost of $500. Major reconditioning is done every 5 years at an average cost of $30,000.[13]

Accessing Wolf Trap Lighthouse is an ambitious undertaking, and can only be accomplished by one who is physically fit and rather nimble. The bow of the boat must be positioned between two round, vertical, rubber bumpers attached to the side of the caisson. The captain must maintain a forward thrust against these bumpers to stabilize the boat. Then the visitor must lunge from the bow of the boat to the lower of two 10 feet ladder sections that are off-set from each other hanging from the wall of the caisson tank. After climbing the upper ladder, entrance to a lower gallery is obtained through a hatch in the exterior, brick-covered deck floor.

The lighthouse consists of the cellar, 2 rooms on the main floor, 3 rooms on the second floor, and a 10' x 12' watch room. From the watch room, a ladder extends up to a trap door in the ceiling that leads to the lantern room. The outhouse hovers over the bay waters from the entrance deck.

The interior and exterior of Wolf Trap were repainted in 1996 by personnel from U.S. Coast Guard ANT Milford Haven, with the assistance of the Coast Guard Auxiliary. Lead-based paint was scraped from the structure. The walls, ceilings, and woodwork of the living quarters have all been freshly painted, and are in a good state of repair. The basement storage area remains in need of cosmetic refurbishing and some minor maintenance. The brick walls suffer from moisture invasion, and are in bad need of repainting. The floors in the living quarters are covered with linoleum block tile that is chipping and cracking and in need of replacement. However, thanks to the efforts of the ANTs, the overall structure has been maintained in an excellent fashion, and Wolf Trap is in excellent condition otherwise.

Wolf Trap Lighthouse was automated in 1971. It is still in operation. It is accessible only by boat, and is not open to the public.

The basement level of Wolf Trap was the only area given no attention during the recent repainting.

[12] de Gast, 39.

[13] de Gast, 39.

Smith Point Lighthouse (1857) is the northern-most lighthouse in the Virginia portion of the Chesapeake Bay.

Access to the off-set lantern room of Smith Point Lighthouse is gained from the small watch room below.

Smith Point Lighthouse

The first lighthouse at Smith Point was an iron frame tower, built in 1802. By 1821, a lightship had been stationed at the point to assist the tower. In 1859, a larger lightship completely replaced the tower. Nine years later, the lightship was replaced by a screwpile lighthouse (1868). In 1895, this lighthouse was destroyed by an ice flow. The **caisson style** lighthouse (**1897**), with its octagonal brick dwelling, is the last of the lighthouses to be placed on this site. It stands in 24 feet of water. It is 52 feet tall.[14]

Although Smith Point and Wolf Trap Lighthouses are similar in design and structure, there are some major differences. Smith Point is illuminated by commercial power provided from underwater cables. If the commercial power is disrupted, a sensoring device activates a switching mechanism that converts to a two 2-volt battery back-up system. This back-up system only operates a smaller emergency light located on the outside of the lantern room until the outage is corrected. The lighthouse is computer linked to ANT Milford Haven in Hudgins and U.S. Coast Guard Group Hampton Roads Engineering at Portsmouth, Virginia. By way of a sophisticated **Automated Monitoring System**, it can provide information about power outages or other necessary repairs. Because of this additional equipment, Smith Point receives routine maintenance every 3 months. The light was automated in 1971.

Smith Point Lighthouse, like Wolf Trap, resembles the average family dwelling of the mid-19th century in design. The outhouse overhangs the deck at the main level. The linoleum block tile on the first floor shows a lot of moisture damage and is chipping and peeling. The walls, floors and ceilings all need to be scraped and repainted. This is costly and time-consuming because of special procedures required to remove the lead-based paint. The Lighthouse contains four levels. The basement walls are lined with brick inside the iron caisson exterior. They are in good condition but most of the paint has peeled and chipped off. The floor is concrete. The entrance level has two larger rooms housing the electronic equipment and the emergency 12-volt battery system. The second floor has three irregular-shaped rooms with tongue and groove wood floors. One interesting feature is a five-sided room with a five-sided closet. The brick walls are covered with tongue and groove wood planks. The window panes have been replaced by plexiglass with ventilator slots. The third floor is an 8'x10' watch room with a metal rung ladder leading through the ceiling and the metal floor of the lantern room. The lantern room is a six feet wide octagonal space enclosed with glass panels. A white light (with a red sector) flashes every 15 seconds from its 1,000-watt light bulb. The lantern has a two-way automatic, rotating lamp changer. A fog signal sounds once every 30 seconds.

As with so many of Virginia's lighthouses, the interior of Smith Point has been neglected due to lack of funds, but the basic structure is sound and in good condition, only needing cosmetic attention.

Smith Point Lighthouse is still active. It is not open to the public, and can only be reached by boat.

Looking down from the second floor, the trap door can been seen , through which supplies and equipment were hoisted to the main levels from the basement.

[14] Holland, *America's Lighthouses*, 116.

Jones Point Lighthouse (1856) is Virginia's only river lighthouse.

The main entrance to Jones Point Lighthouse overlooks the waters of the Potomac River.

Jones Point Lighthouse

Sitting on a knoll in Alexandria, just yards from the edge of the waters of the Potomac, is the last of the river lighthouses to be found in the state of Virginia. Jones Point Lighthouse, a small structure covered with English siding, rests on a brick foundation. It was completed in **1856.** The building is only 772 square feet. At one time, however, the dwelling housed the entire Greenwood family, which consisted of the parents and eleven children.

The site offers a beautiful and tranquil setting of overhanging trees, grassy fields, picnic tables, bicycle and walking trails, and wooded areas that line the banks of the Potomac River. The lighthouse sits nestled picturesquely on a fifty-acre tract of land developed as a public park by the National Park Service. Sailboats, motor boats, river barges, and tour boats pass within just a few yards of the lighthouse.

Mid-way between the swinging gate in the newly-constructed picket fence (built to replicate the one on the site in the 1940s) and the lighthouse is a six feet square, masonry foundation that once supported the covered well from which the family obtained its drinking, bathing, washing, and cooking water. The well has long since been filled in with dirt. There was once a wood walkway from the well to the door that appears to be the front door. However, the "front door" is the door facing the Potomac River. This door is larger and was flanked by 7' vertical lights (panels of glass) on each side.

A central hallway separates two large rooms on the main floor, with a hatch door in the center of the hallway leading to the basement. Each room has a large brick hearth and fireplace on the outside wall, with inbound (interior) chimneys. Both fireplaces have been destroyed and need to be completely rebuilt.

There is one large room above the main floor with a pitched dormer-style ceiling. Only a small area of the tongue and groove floorboards remains in this room. Vagrants, who once took up residence in the lighthouse, burned a 3' in diameter hole in this area of the floor. The lantern room is accessed from the second story by a ladder extending through a sixteen-inch square opening in the ceiling. The interior of the lantern room resembles a large barrel. Tongue and groove plank boards line the circular room up to ten trapezoidal storm panes containing finger-like ventilator slots. The lantern was originally fueled by whale oil, and later converted to acetylene gas. Commercial electricity is now supplied through an underground service line that provides power to the lamp. The light is controlled by a photo-electric cell that automatically illuminates the lamp at dusk and extinguishes it at dawn. A white light flashes every four seconds. The bulbs are contained in a six-bulb lamp changer that automatically rotates to another bulb when one burns out. The lighthouse is now listed as a private aid to navigation. Scant, conduit-enclosed wiring provides temporary power to the remainder of the lighthouse.

The exterior of the lantern room is constructed of metal plates, and is painted gray. The gallery on the outside of the lantern room has been removed. An iron pipe handrail, with no platform (gallery), surrounds the lantern room that extends through the cedar shake roof from the center of the dwelling.

The basement is accessed by way of a hatch door in the floor of the main hallway. The basement walls and floors are made of brick. Traces of the old whitewash remains on the walls in the front room that was used as the winter kitchen. The floors were left unpainted. A hearth and fireplace nest in each of these rooms, directly under the ones located on the main floor. The outside basement entrance has been closed with cinder block.

The interior walls and floors of the lighthouse, from the main floor to the roof, have all been torn out and gutted. Only the wall studs and floor joists remain in most of the interior space. The exterior of the lighthouse has been repaired, newly painted, and is in excellent condition. The site is attractive and well maintained.

Rip rap has been placed in front of the sea wall for protection from the waters of the river. Jones Point Lighthouse was one of the few dwellings of the era to have an automatic sewage disposal system. At one time, the buoy house also served as the outhouse, and sat within the fenced in area of the yard. There was a tunnel that led from the outhouse to the river by way of an opening in the sea wall. During high tide, the water from the river would flow into the tunnel, providing a "tidal flush" of the waste materials from the outhouse. The opening in the sea wall still remains.

Near the front door (facing the Potomac), the original boundary marker of the District of Columbia is visible if one looks down through a hole in the top of the sea wall. It is dated April 15, 1791. Fifty-three feet from the back of the lighthouse is another marker designating the boundary for the State of Maryland. One can actually walk from Virginia into Maryland from this point and stroll along the river bank of our adjoining state.

Since the early 1900s, the Daughters of the American Revolution has had actual deeded ownership of, or a vested interest in the welfare of, Jones Point Lighthouse. The lighthouse is now the property of the National Park Service, and this organization has agreed to maintain and interpret the lighthouse, once it is repaired, until the year 2016. National Park Service personnel estimate the cost of restoring the structure to be around $150,000. The mutual goal of the groups is to make the lighthouse accessible to the public for viewing and interpretation. An initial step will be a structural assessment by engineers to determine necessary repairs to open the dwelling to the public on a non-restricted basis. If this is too costly, opening the lighthouse on a restricted basis is an option being considered. Whichever option proves to be financially feasible, the reconstruction and public viewing of Jones Point Lighthouse seems to be a very real possibility for the near future.

Jones Point Lighthouse is a definite study in contrasts. The exterior of the lighthouse has been repaired, repainted, and is in excellent condition. The interior is in total disarray and in need of complete restoration, with only the shell of the structure remaining. The lighthouse is not open to the public. However, a walk-around visit is possible. The light does, once again, shine thanks to the National Park Service and the efforts of the Mount Vernon Chapter of the Daughters of the American Revolution.

A visit to Jones Point Lighthouse also puts one in close proximity to the many tourist attractions our National Capital has to offer. Many of the motels and hotels in the area offer shuttle services to the Metro (the subway system for the Capital area). Easy travel to all the attractions is possible with this convenient source of transportation.

To reach Jones Point Lighthouse, take Interstate 495, 95 (Capital Beltway). Exit the Beltway onto State Route 1. Turn right onto Franklin Street. Turn right onto South Royal Street. At the Jones Point Army Reserve Building, turn right under the bridge at column marker 13W. Turn left on Jones Point Road at the entrance to Jones Point Park.

The four hearths that were originally found in Jones Point Lighthouse provided cooking areas and heat for the keeper and his family.

Bibliography

Adams, William Henry Davenport. *Lighthouses and Lightships: A Descriptive and Historical Account of Their Mode of Construction and Organization.* New York: Scribner's, 1870.

Brown, Alexander Crosby. "Wolf Trap Shoal," *Chesapeake Skipper*, April, 1951.

Burgess, Robert H. *This Was Chesapeake Bay.* Cambridge, Md.: Cornell Maritime Press, 1965.

de Gast, Robert. *The Lighthouses of The Chesapeake.* Baltimore, Md.: The Johns Hopkins University Press, 1973.

Dorsey, Jack. "Old Cape Henry Lighthouse May Gleam as Beach Signal," *The Ledger Star,* August 26, 1965.

Harris, Bill. *Lighthouses of America.* New York, New York: Crescent Books, 1991.

Hatch, Jr., Charles. *The Old Cape Henry Light.* (pamphlet) Virginia Beach, Virginia: Association for the Preservation of Virginia Antiquities.

Holland, F. Ross, Jr. *Great American Lighthouses.* Washington, D.C.: The Preservation Press, 1989.

Holland, F. Ross, Jr. *America's Lighthouses, An Illustrated History.* New York, New York: Dover Publications, Inc., 1972.

Naush, John M. *Seamarks: Their History and Development.* London: Stanford Maritime, 1985.

Putnam, George R. *Lighthouses and Lightships of the United States.* Boston: Houghton Mifflin, 1917.

Pouliot, Richard, and Julie. *Shipwrecks on the Virginia Coast.* Centerville, Md.: Tidewater, 1986.

Roberts, B. and Jones, R. SOUTHERN LIGHTHOUSES: *Chesapeake Bay to the Gulf of Mexico.* Old Saybrook, Connecticut: Globe Pequot Press, 1995.

Roberts, B. and Jones, R. MID-ATLANTIC LIGHTHOUSES: *Hudson River to Chesapeake Bay.* Old Saybrook, Connecticut: Globe Pequot Press, 1996.

Shanklin, B.and S. *Bob and Sandra Shanklin's List of All Existing U.S. Lighthouses.* 2nd ed. 1993.

Snow, Edward R. *Famous Lighthouses of America.* New York: Dodd, Mead, 1955.

Spatuzzi, John. *Beautiful Lighthouses.* Davie, Florida: Horizon Images, 1994.

Turbeyville, Linda. Bay Beacons: *Lighthouse of the Chesapeake Bay.* Annapolis, Md.: Eastwind Publishing, 1995.

Index

Aids to Navigation Teams (ANTs), 3, 6
Ambrose Lightship, 19
ANT Chincoteague, 12
ANT Kennebec, 5, 6
ANT Milford Haven, 5, 6, 33, 35
Argand reflector, 17
Assateague Island, 11
Assateague Island Lighthouse, 7, 10, 11
Association for the Preservation of Virginia Antiquities, 15
Automated Monitoring Control System (AMC), 14, 35
Caisson, 9, 25, 29, 35
Cape Charles Lighthouse, 7, 11, 13, 23
Cape Henry Lighthouse, 14, 15
New Cape Henry Lighthouse, 17
Characteristic, 9
Chesapeake Bay, 7, 17, 33
Chesapeake Lighthouse, 7, 19
Chincoteague Island, 12
Civil War, (War Between the States), 11, 13, 15, 33
Coast Guard Auxiliary, 5, 6, 33
Coast Guard List, 2
Conical tower, 9
Day marks, 9
Daylight Control Monitoring System, 11
Diamond Shoals Lighthouse, 19
Fifth Coast Guard District, 3, 5, 6
Fresnel lens, 11, 13, 17, 23
Frying Pan Shoals Lighthouse, 19
Global Positioning System (GPS), 17
Jones Point Lighthouse, 7, 37
LV 102, 23
Lightship Charles, 23
Lightship Portsmouth (LV 101), 7, 23
New Cape Henry Lighthouse, 7, 11
New Point Comfort Lighthouse, 7, 31
Newport News Middle Ground Lighthouse, 7, 24, 25
Octagonal tower, 9, 15, 31
Old Point Comfort Lighthouse, 7, 27, 31
Olympia, 22
Potomac River, 35, 37
Primary light, 11, 17
Secondary light, 11, 17
Skeletal tower, 9, 13
Smith Island, 13
Smith Point Lighthouse, 7, 23, 35
Texas Tower, 19
Thimble Shoals Lighthouse, 7, 29
Vega Rotating Beacon (VRB), 13, 19
Whale-back hull, 23
Wolf Trap Lighthouse, 7, 33, 35

About the Author

    Jerry Zaccaria was born near Philadelphia, Pennsylvania. His preteen years were spent in the suburban community of Holmes, just 60 miles from Atlantic City, New Jersey. He and his family spent the summers at their vacation house, just blocks from the then famous Steel Pier and Captain Starn's Restaurant on the world renowned Atlantic City Board Walk. The daily trips to the beach led him past the Absecon Lighthouse. In the evenings, he sat on the front porch of his family's summer house, watching the flash of the areobeacon that had replaced the discontinued lighthouse skip across the rooftops of the neighborhood houses. During these many summers, swimming and growing up around the shore, and enjoying the excitement of the beach life, "salt water and sand got into my blood." It remains to this day. When he was fourteen, his family relocated to Staunton, in the Shenandoah Valley of Virginia, home of the popular country quartet, The Statler Brothers. He earned a Bachelor of Science in Education degree from Madison College, and a Master of Education in School Administration degree from James Madison University, both in Harrisonburg, Virginia. His career as a professional educator consisted of eighteen years as an elementary school teacher and fifteen years as an elementary school administrator. Jerry is a member of the Lighthouse Preservation Society, The United States Lighthouse Society, and the Chesapeake Chapter of the United States Lighthouse Society.

    The Zaccarias have two grown children, Tamara and Greg. Their two younger children, Leigh Ann and Anna, have spent the past five years touring, photographing, and studying lighthouses along the major portion of the east coast with Jerry and his wife, Edna.

    During the writing of this book, Jerry spent four months traveling with the ANTs of the Fifth Coast Guard District, visiting and photographing all the lighthouses of Virginia. The author's retirement dream is to spend the rest of his life at the shore, where he can sit in his back yard and enjoy the flash of the lighthouse and the sound of the surf rolling toward the beach, or perhaps... to even live in a lighthouse!

Appendix

Chronological Listing of Virginia's Lighthouses

1792 Old Cape Henry	President George Washington	1789-97 *
1802 Old Point Comfort	President Thomas Jefferson	1801-09 *
1805 New Point Comfort	President Thomas Jefferson	1801-09
1856 Jones Point	President Franklin Pierce	1853-57
1867 Assateague (1833)	President Andrew Johnson	1865-69
1881 New Cape Henry	President Chester A. Arthur	1881-85
1891 Middle Ground	President Benjamin Harrison	1889-93
1894 Wolf Trap (1870)	President Grover Cleveland	1893-97
1895 Cape Charles (1828, 1864)	President Grover Cleveland	1893-97
1897 Smith Point (1802, 1807, 1828, 1868)	President Grover Cleveland	1893-97
1914 Thimble Shoal (1872, 1880)	President Woodrow Wilson	1913-21 *
1916 Lightship Portmouth	President Woodrow Wilson	1913-21
1965 Chesapeake	President Lyndon Johnson	1963-69

* Virginia Presidents

Photographers

Beth Trainum is an award winning professional photographer who lives in Staunton, Virginia. She owns and operates her own studio and works on commission, with special emphasis on portraiture, landscape, and architecture. Beth enjoys every photographic challenge; the light and texture of a peaceful landscape; the structural detail of a towering building; capturing the personality of a child, or the romantic ambiance of a young bride. Beth is well known for her dedication to her subjects, and takes a great deal of pride in producing quality photographs. Beth lives with "camera in hand", and is always ready for that special photographic moment. She has traveled from coast to coast, taking photographs both professionally and for personal pleasure. As a result of her involvement with this book, Beth has become an avid lighthouse lover. Ms. Trainum also works as a school photographer for a well-established firm based in Durham, North Carolina.

Danielle McMillion began taking pictures in high school, where she served as her school's yearbook photographer. After completing photography courses at Blue Ridge Community College in Weyers Cave, Virginia, she began her professional career as a news photographer for the Daily News Leader in Staunton, Virginia. Danielle is now a free-lance photographer whose work has covered a wide range of interests, including news events, sports events, portrait photography, wedding photography, aerial photography, landscapes, seascapes, and speciality assignments in the operating room for surgeons. She is the recipient of the Virginia Press Association State Award for Combination Sequent Series Photography. She lives in Stuarts Draft, Virginia with her husband, Michael, and three children, Aaron, Kaitlyn, and Emily, who are her favorite photographic subjects.